INTRODUCTION

Welcome back to FastTrack™!

Hope you enjoyed Keyboard 2 and are ready to play some hits. Have you and your friends formed a band? Or do you feel like soloing with the CD? Either way, make sure you're relaxed and turned up loud…it's time to jam!

As always, don't try to bite off more than you can chew. If your hands hurt, take some time off. If you get frustrated, turn off your keyboard, sit back and just listen to the CD. If you forget a technique, rhythm, or note position, go back and learn it. If you're doing fine, think about finding an agent.

CONTENTS

CD Track	Song Title	Page
1	All Day and All of the Night	4
2	Best of My Love	6
3	Day Tripper	11
4	Hey Joe	14
5	I Shot the Sheriff	17
6	Miss You	19
7	Smoke on the Water	25
8	Surfin' U.S.A.	28

ABOUT THE CD

Again, you get a CD with the book! Each song in the book is included on the CD, so you can hear how it sounds and play along when you're ready.

Each example on the CD is preceded by one measure of "clicks" to indicate the tempo and meter. Pan right to hear the keyboard part emphasized. Pan left to hear the accompaniment emphasized.

HAL•LEONARD® CORPORATION
7777 W. BLUEMOUND RD. P.O. BOX 13819 MILWAUKEE, WI 53213

Visit Hal Leonard online at
www.halleonard.comwww.halleonard.com

LEARN SOMETHING NEW EACH DAY

We know you're eager to play, but first we need to explain a few new things. We'll make it brief—only one page...

Melody and Lyrics

There's that extra musical staff again! In **Keyboard 1 Songbook**, sometimes you or the guitar player were actually playing the melody. But in this songbook, each instrument has its own accompaniment part (more like a real band would!).

The additional staff on top shows you the song's melody and lyrics. This way, you can follow along more easily as you play your accompaniment part, whether it's chords or harmony or a blazing solo.

And if you happen to be playing with a singer, this new staff is their part.

Endings

In case you've forgotten some of the **ending symbols** from *Songbook 1*, here's a reminder:

1st and 2nd Endings

These are indicated by brackets and numbers:

Simply play the song through to the first ending, then repeat back to the first repeat sign, or beginning of the song (whichever is the case). Play through the song again, but skip the first ending and play the second ending.

D.S. al Coda

When you see these words, go back and repeat from this symbol: 𝄋

Play until you see the words *"To Coda"* then skip to the Coda, indicated by this symbol: 𝄌

Now just finish the song.

New Chord

When you play "Best of My Love," you'll notice two new chord types, a major seventh (maj7) and a minor sixth (m6).

Don't panic! To play a major seventh, simply raise the seventh of the C7 or F7 by one half step. That is, play C-E-G-B or F-A-C-E (hey, it spells "face"!) instead of the B-flat or E-flat normally found in a "7" chord.

For the Fm6 (F minor sixth), play an F minor chord and add a sixth (D) on top, so that you're playing the notes F-A flat-C-D.

That's about it! Enjoy the music...

◆ 1 All Day and All of the Night

Words and Music by Ray Davies

Intro
Moderate Rock ♩ = 138

Verse

not con - tent to be with you in the day - time.
2., 3. I be - lieve to that you and me last for - ev - er.

Girl, I want to be with you all of the ___
Oh, yeah, all day and night I'm yours. Leave me nev -

Pre-Chorus

___ time.
- er.

The on - ly time I

feel al - right is by your ___ side. ___

Chorus

Girl, I want to be with you all of the ___ time. All day and all of the night. ___

To Coda ⊕

All day and all of the night. _ All day and all of the night. _

2.

Oh, come on!

Guitar Solo   *D.S. al Coda*

⊕ *Coda*

All day and all of the night. _

Best of My Love

Words and Music by John David Souther, Don Henley and Glenn Frey

Intro
Moderately Slow ♩ = 92

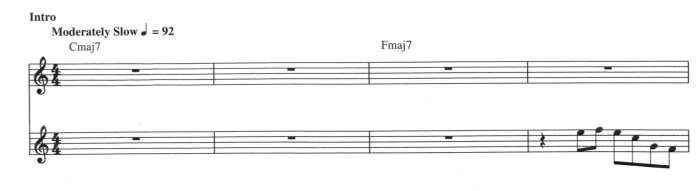

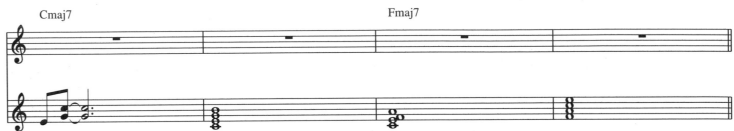

Verse

1. Ev - er - y night __ I'm ly - in' in bed, ___ hold - in' you close __ in my

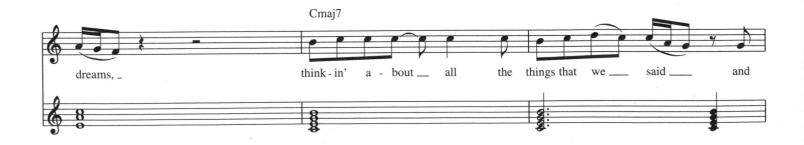

dreams, _ think - in' a - bout __ all the things that we ___ said ___ and

com - in' a - part ___ at the seams. ___ We tried to talk it o -

-ver but the words come out __ too __ rough. __ I

know you were try - in' to give me the best _ of your _ love.

Verse

2. Beau - ti - ful fa - ces and loud emp - ty pla - ces, look at the way that we

live. __ Wast - in' our time __ on cheap talk and wine __

left us so lit - tle to give. __ That same old __ crowd __ was like a

cold dark cloud ___ that we could nev-er rise a-bove. ___ But

here in my heart ___ I give you the best ___ of my ___ love. Oh, _____

Chorus

___ sweet dar - lin, you get the best of my
(You get the best of my ___ love.)

love. ___ Oh, _____ sweet dar - lin', ___
(You get the best of my love. ___

Bridge

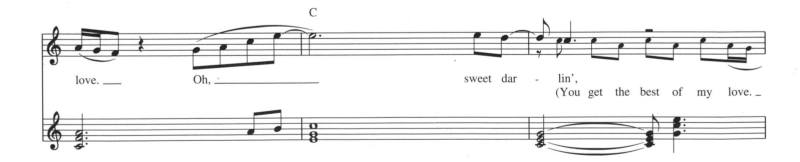

you get the best of my ___ love. I'm go-in' back in time ___ and it's a
___)

Outro-Chorus

10

Day Tripper

Words and Music by John Lennon and Paul McCartney

Interlude

N.C.

E

D.S. al Coda

𝄌 *Coda*

Interlude

N.C.

E

Outro

E

Day trip-per.

Day trip-per, yeah. __

Day trip-per.

Day trip-per, yeah. __

Hey Joe

Words and Music by Billy Roberts

Verse

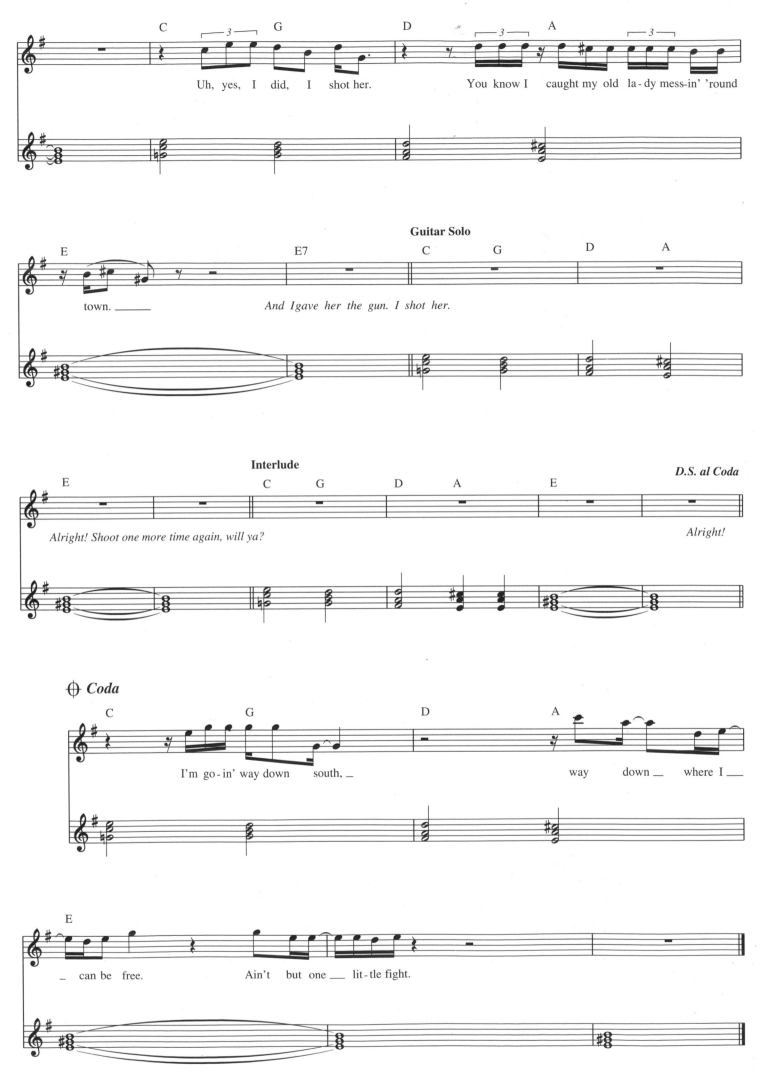

Uh, yes, I did, I shot her. You know I caught my old la-dy mess-in' 'round town. _____

And I gave her the gun. I shot her.

Guitar Solo

Interlude

D.S. al Coda

Alright! Shoot one more time again, will ya? *Alright!*

⊕ Coda

I'm go-in' way down south, _ way down _ where I _

_ can be free. Ain't but one _ lit-tle fight.

⬥5 I Shot the Sheriff

Words and Music by Bob Marley

Intro · **Moderate Reggae** ♩ = 94 · **Chorus**

1. I shot the sher-iff
2. I shot the sher-iff
3.-4. *See Additional Lyrics*

but I did not shoot the dep-u-ty.
but I swear it was in self de-fense.

I shot the sher-iff
I shot the sher-iff

but I did-n't shoot the dep-u-ty.
and they say it is a cap-i-tal of-fense.

Verse

All a-round in my home-town
Sher-iff John Brown al-ways hat-ed me,

they're try-in' to track me down. ___
for what I don't know. ___

Additional Lyrics

3. I shot the sheriff
   But I swear it was in self-defense.
   I shot the sheriff
   But I swear it was in self-defense.
   Freedom came my way one day
   And I started out down there.
   All of a sudden I see sheriff John Brown.
   Aiming to shoot me down.
   So I shot, I shot him down.
   And I say...

4. I shot the sheriff
   But I did not shoot the deputy.
   I shot the sheriff
   But I didn't shoot the deputy.
   Reflexes got the better of me.
   And what is to be must be.
   Every day the bucket goes to the well,
   But one day the bottom will drop out.
   Yes, one day the bottom will drop out.
   And I say...

Miss You

Words and Music by Mick Jagger and Keith Richards

Chorus

Ooh. Ooh. Ooh.

Ooh. Ooh. 2. Well, I've been haunt-

Verse

_____ ing in __ my sleep. You been star - in' in __ my dream. _ Lord, I miss you, child.

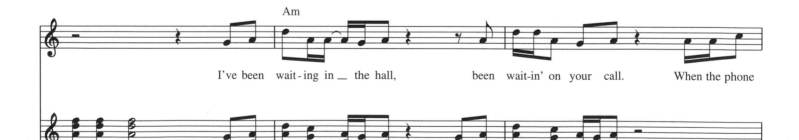

I've been wait-ing in __ the hall, been wait-in' on your call. When the phone

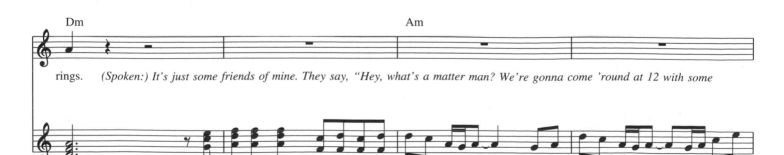

rings. *(Spoken:) It's just some friends of mine. They say, "Hey, what's a matter man? We're gonna come 'round at 12 with some*

20

Puerto Rican girls that's just dyin' to meet you! We're gonna bring a case of wine. Hey, let's go mess and fool around.

Chorus

You know, like we used to!"

Ah. _____ Ah. _____ Ah. ___

Ah. _____ Ah. _____ Ah. ___

Bridge

Oh, oh, oh. Ba - by why you wait so long? _

Oh, oh, oh. Ba - by why you wait so long? _

Interlude

Won't you come home? Come home! Ah.

Ti - ki - ti ti - ki - ti ti - ki - ti ti - ki. I've been walk-ing Cen - tral Park,

sing-ing af - ter dark. Peo-ple think I'm cra - zy.

Stumb-ling on my feet, shuf-flin' to the street, ask-ing peo - ple ch - ch - ch

what's a mat-ter with you, boy? Some - time I wan-na say to, to my-

Outro-Chorus

7 Smoke on the Water

Words and Music by Ritchie Blackmore, Ian Gillan, Roger Glover, Jon Lord and Ian Paice

We did - n't have much time. ___ But Frank Zap - pa and the
pull - ing kids off the ground. When it all was
mak - ing our mu - sic there. With a few red lights, a

Moth - ers ___ were at the best place a - round. ___
o - ver ___ we had to find an - oth - er place. ___
few old beds, we made a place to sweat. ___

But some stu - pid with a flare gun burned the place to the ground. ___
The Swiss time was run - ning out. It seemed that we would lose the race. ___
No mat - ter what we get out of this, I know, I know we'll never for - get. ___

Chorus

Smoke on the wat - er, a fi - re in the sky. ___

Smoke on the wat - er.

To Coda ⊕

Guitar Solo

Gm   Cm7   Gm   C5

F   N.C.   *D.S. al Coda*

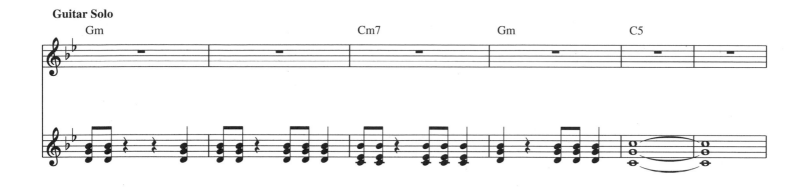

⊕ *Coda*

Surfin' U.S.A.

Written by Chuck Berry and Brian Wilson

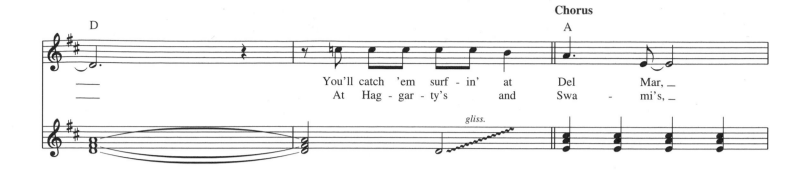

Chorus

You'll catch 'em surf - in' at Del Mar, ___
At Hag - gar - ty's and Swa - mi's, ___

Ven - tu - ra Coun - ty Line, ___ San - ta Cruz and Tress - els, ___
Pa - ci - fic Pal - i - sades, ___ San O - no - fre and Sun - set, ___

Aus - tra - lia's Nar - a - bine. ___ All o - ver Man - hat - tan
Re - don - do Beach L. A. ___ All o - ver La Jol - la ___

and down Do - he - ny way. ___ Ev - 'ry - bod - y's gone surf - in', ___
at Wal - a - me - a Bay. ___

Keyboard Solo

(1st time only)

surf - in' U. S. A. ___ 2. We'll all be plan - ning out a

(2nd time only)

29

Guitar Solo

Ev - 'ry-bod-y's gone

gliss.

Outro-Chorus

surf - in', ___ Surf-in' U. S. A. ___ Ev - 'ry-bod-y's gone

surf - in', ___ surf-in' U. S. A. ___ Ev - 'ry-bod-y's gone

surf - in', ___ surf-in' U. S. A. ___

FastTrack is (you guessed it!) a fast way for beginners to learn to play that instrument they just bought. **FastTrack** is different from other method books: we've made them user-friendly with plenty of cool songs (by The Beatles, Eric Clapton, Elton John and other great artists!) that make it easy and fun for players to teach themselves. Plus, the last section of all the **FastTrack** books have the same songs so that students can form a band and jam together. Songbooks are all compatible, and feature eight songs. **Songbook 1 – Level 1** includes: You Really Got Me • Wild Thing • I Want To Hold Your Hand • Brown Eyed Girl • Oh, Pretty Woman • and more. **Songbook 2 – Level 1** includes: Evil Ways • Gimme Some Lovin' • Gloria • Twist and Shout • and more. **Songbook 1 – Level 2** includes: Back in the U.S.S.R. • Born to Be Wild • Layla • Maggie May • Takin' Care of Business • and more. **Songbook 2 – Level 2** includes: Hey Joe • I Shot the Sheriff • Smoke on the Water • Surfin' U.S.A. • and more. All packs include a great play-along CD with professional-sounding back-up band.

FASTTRACK GUITAR

For Electric or Acoustic Guitar – or both!
by Blake Neely & Jeff Schroedl
Teaches music notation, tablature, full chords and power chords, riffs, licks, and scales, and rock and blues styles. Method Book 1 includes 73 songs and examples.

METHOD BOOK 1
00697282 Book/CD Pack..$7.95

SONGBOOK 1 – LEVEL 1
00697287 Book/CD Pack......................................$12.95

SONGBOOK 2 – LEVEL 1
00695343 Book/CD Pack......................................$12.95

CHORDS & SCALES
00697291 Book/CD Pack..$9.95

METHOD BOOK 2
00697286 Book/CD Pack..$9.95

SONGBOOK 1 – LEVEL 2
00697296 Book/CD Pack......................................$12.95

SONGBOOK 2 – LEVEL 2
00695344 Book/CD Pack......................................$12.95

FASTTRACK BASS

by Blake Neely & Jeff Schroedl
Everything you need to know about playing the bass, including music notation, tablature, riffs, licks, and scales, syncopation, and rock and blues styles. Method Book 1 includes 75 songs and examples.

METHOD BOOK 1
00697284 Book/CD Pack..$7.95

SONGBOOK 1 – LEVEL 1
00697289 Book/CD Pack......................................$12.95

SONGBOOK 2 – LEVEL 1
00695368 Book/CD Pack......................................$12.95

METHOD BOOK 2
00697294 Book/CD Pack..$9.95

SONGBOOK 1 LEVEL 2
00697298 Book/CD Pack......................................$12.95

SONGBOOK 2 LEVEL 2
00695368 Book/CD Pack......................................$12.95

FASTTRACK KEYBOARD

For Electric Keyboard, Synthesizer, or Piano
by Blake Neely & Gary Meisner
Learn how to play that piano today. With this book you'll learn music notation, chords, riffs, licks and scales, syncopation, and rock and blues styles. Method Book 1 includes over 87 songs and examples.

METHOD BOOK 1
00697283 Book/CD Pack..$7.95

SONGBOOK 1 – LEVEL 1
00697288 Book/CD Pack......................................$12.95

SONGBOOK 2 – LEVEL 1
00695366 Book/CD Pack......................................$12.95

CHORDS & SCALES
00697292 Book/CD Pack..$9.95

METHOD BOOK 2
00697293 Book/CD Pack..$9.95

SONGBOOK 1 LEVEL 2
00697297 Book/CD Pack......................................$12.95

SONGBOOK 2 LEVEL 2
00695366 Book/CD Pack......................................$12.95

FASTTRACK SAXOPHONE

by Blake Neely
With this book, you'll learn music notation; riffs, scales, keys; syncopation; rock and blues styles; and includes 72 songs and examples.

METHOD BOOK 1
00695241 Book/CD Pack $7.95

FASTTRACK DRUMS

by Blake Neely & Rick Mattingly
With this book, you'll learn music notation, riffs and licks, syncopation, rock, blues and funk styles, and improvisation. Method Book 1 includes over 75 songs and examples.

METHOD BOOK 1
00697285 Book/CD Pack......................................$7.95

SONGBOOK 1 – LEVEL 1
00697290 Book/CD Pack......................................$12.95

SONGBOOK 2 – LEVEL 1
00695367 Book/CD Pack......................................$12.95

METHOD BOOK TWO
00697295 Book/CD Pack......................................$9.95

SONGBOOK 1 LEVEL 2
00697299 Book/CD Pack......................................$12.95

SONGBOOK 2 LEVEL 2
00695367 Book/CD Pack......................................$12.95

FOR MORE INFORMATION, SEE YOUR LOCAL MUSIC DEALER, OR WRITE TO:

HAL•LEONARD® CORPORATION
7777 W. BLUEMOUND RD. P.O. BOX 13819 MILWAUKEE, WI 53213

Prices, contents, and availability subject to change without notice. Some products may not be available outside the U.S.A.

0799